COLLECTING DATA
Pick a Pancake

Based on the Math Monsters™ public television series, developed in cooperation with the National Council of Teachers of Mathematics (NCTM).

by John Burstein

Reading consultant: Susan Nations, M.Ed., author/literacy coach/consultant
Math curriculum consultants: Marti Wolfe, M.Ed., teacher/presenter; Kristi Hardi-Gilson, B.A., teacher/presenter

WEEKLY WR READER®
EARLY LEARNING LIBRARY

Please visit our web site at: **www.earlyliteracy.cc**
For a free color catalog describing Weekly Reader® Early Learning Library's list
of high-quality books, call 1-877-445-5824 (USA) or 1-800-387-3178 (Canada).
Weekly Reader® Early Learning Library's fax: (414) 336-0164.

Library of Congress Cataloging-in-Publication Data

Burstein, John.
    Collecting data: pick a pancake / by John Burstein.
        p. cm. — (Math monsters)
    Summary: The four math monsters show how to collect and chart data as they help Addison
figure out what kind of pancakes he should sell in his shop.
    ISBN 0-8368-3805-X (lib. bdg.)
    ISBN 0-8368-3820-3 (softcover)
    1. Statistics—Graphic methods—Juvenile literature. [1. Statistics—Graphic methods.] I. Title.
QA276.3.B87   2003
001.4'33—dc21
                                                                            2003045011

This edition first published in 2004 by
Weekly Reader® Early Learning Library
330 West Olive Street, Suite 100
Milwaukee, WI 53212 USA

Text and artwork copyright © 2004 by Slim Goodbody Corp. (www.slimgoodbody.com).
This edition copyright © 2004 by Weekly Reader® Early Learning Library.

Original Math Monsters™ animation: Destiny Images
Art direction, cover design, and page layout: Tammy Gruenewald
Editor: JoAnn Early Macken

Printed in the United States of America

1 2 3 4 5 6 7 8 9 07 06 05 04 03

You can enrich children's mathematical experience by working with
them as they tackle the Corner Questions in this book. Create
a special notebook for recording their mathematical ideas.

Data and Math

Data collection serves as a wonderful opportunity for young children
to experiment with multiple representations of the same information.
This is a key concept in mathematics.

Meet the Math Monsters™

Addison thinks
math is fun.
"I solve problems
one by one."

ADDISON

Mina flies
from here to there.
"I look for answers
everywhere."

MINA

Multiplex
sure loves to laugh.
"Both my heads
have fun with math."

MULTIPLEX

Split is friendly
as can be.
"If you need help,
then count on me."

SPLIT

We're glad you want to take a look
at the story in our book.

We know that as you read, you'll see
just how helpful math can be.

Let's get started. Jump right in!
Turn the page, and let's begin!

Addison loved to cook. He made very good
pancakes. He sang,
　"Flip them up.
　They come back down.
　My pancakes are
　the best in town."

"Mmm, mmm!" said Multiplex.
"These taste great."

"Let's open a pancake shop,"
said Split.

What is your favorite food for breakfast?

5

The Math Monsters talked about the kinds of pancakes they might sell in their shop.

"We can sell banana pancakes," said Split.

"We can sell blueberry pancakes," said Mina.

"We can sell bubble gum pancakes," said Multiplex, "and spinach pancakes, too."

"I only have three mixing bowls," said Addison. "We can only sell three kinds of pancakes."

"Which three?" asked Split.

"We need to find out what kind of pancakes most of our monster friends like," said Mina.

What can the monsters do to find out?

"I have an idea," said Addison. "Let's each ask ten
friends to tell us what kind of pancakes they like best."

"We can find out what each friend likes. We can mark it down on paper," said Mina.

"Then we will have all the data we need," said Split.

"What is data?" asked Multiplex.

What do you think data is?

"Our data will be the facts we collect," said Addison.
"This data will show us what our monster friends
like best."

"Let's go find out right now!" said Multiplex.

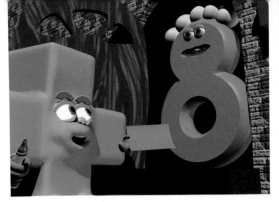

Addison asked ten friends.

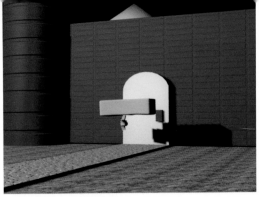

Mina did, too.

Split went to ten homes.

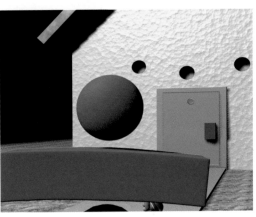

So did Multiplex.

If each monster asks ten friends, how many friends will they ask in all?

The monsters came back home to their castle.
Addison said, "We have data from forty friends."
"Let's share the facts we learned," said Mina.

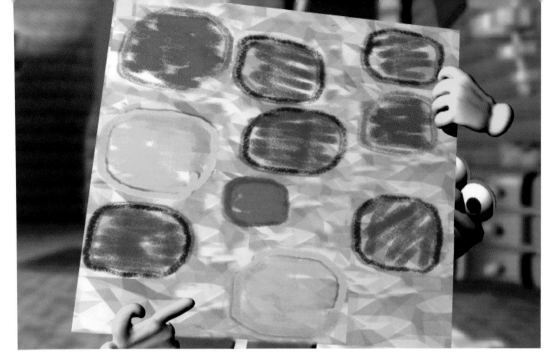

Multiplex went first.

"I put my data in a picture," he said. "My friends told me what kinds of pancakes they like best. I drew them right here. I gave each kind its own color. Blue is for blueberry. Red is for bubble gum. Yellow is for banana. Green is for spinach."

Can you tell what kind of pancakes most of Multiplex's friends like best?

"My data shows that most of my friends like blueberry pancakes best," said Multiplex.

Addison showed the other monsters his data.

"I drew my pancakes in stacks," he said. "The stack of pink bubble gum pancakes is the tallest. That means most of my friends like bubble gum pancakes best."

Do you agree? Do Addison's friends like bubble gum best?

"Wait," said Mina. "The bubble gum pile has only two pancakes. The spinach pile has four."

"Oops," said Addison. "I drew the bubble gum pancakes too big. Now I can see that most of my friends like spinach best."

Dextris Digit	BLUEBERRY
Ivan Idea	BLUEBERRY
Al Gorythm	SPINACH
Noah Number	BUBBLE GUM
Dee Cipher	SPINACH
Ima Fraction	BUBBLE GUM
May Trix	SPINACH
Algie Bra	BLUEBERRY
Ann Sir	BLUEBERRY
Mat O'Matics	BANANA

Split shared her data next.

"I made a list of names," she said. "Next to each name, I wrote the kind of pancakes each monster likes best."

What kind of pancakes do most of Split's friends like best?

"Most of your friends like blueberry best," said Mina. "Now I will show you my data."

Mina held up her paper.

"I listed the kinds of pancakes on the side," she said. Each time a friend told me which kind he or she liked best, I put a check mark next to it."

Do you think Mina has found a good way to show her data? Why?

"Your data is very easy to read," said Addison. "I can see right away that your friends like bubble gum and banana best."

"My data does not show the same thing as your data," said Split.

"What do you mean?" asked Mina.

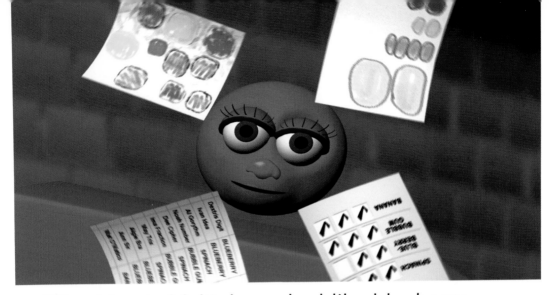

"The friends Multiplex asked like blueberry pancakes best. My friends did, too. Addison's friends like spinach. Mina's friends like bubble gum and banana."

"We need to put all of our data together," said Addison. "Then we can see it at the same time. We will know what all of our friends like best."

"How can we do that?" asked Multiplex.

How can the monsters put all their data together?

21

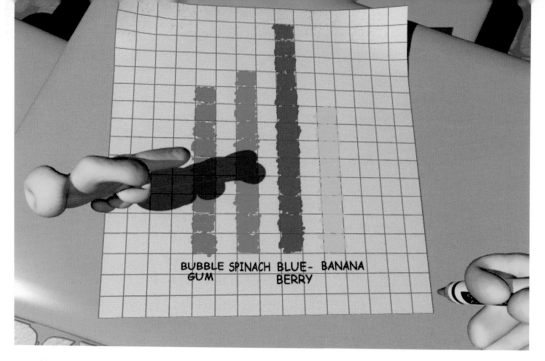

BUBBLE SPINACH BLUE- BANANA
GUM   BERRY

"We can put all the data in a graph," said Mina.
"On the bottom, we can list the pancakes. Then we
can color in boxes above the names. We can color
in one box for each monster who likes that kind."

One by one, the monsters used their data to fill in
the graph.

"Blueberry has the most boxes colored in. Next
comes bubble gum," said Mina. "Spinach comes
in third."

In the pancake shop, Addison made the three
kinds of pancakes most monsters liked best.

The monsters sang,

"We went north, east, south, and west,

all through Monster Town,

to find out what our friends liked best.

This is what we found:

The pancakes most friends

want to chew

are blueberry, spinach,

and bubble gum, too."

*What other
reasons do
people have for
collecting data?*

ACTIVITIES

Page 5 See what kind of answers children come up with. Discuss the importance of eating a good breakfast.

Page 7 Discuss a similar situation. What if you were having a pizza party and could only serve three kinds of pizza? Discuss how children would find out what their friends liked best.

Page 9 Data is another word for facts, figures, or information. Give an example. Remind children that every time they see a doctor, data is collected about their height, weight, and other health factors. Teachers collect data when they take attendance each day.

Page 11 This is a good opportunity to practice counting by tens.

Page 13 Ask your children if they can show a better way to group Multiplex's data. Provide crayons and paper.

Pages 15, 17, 19 For each chart, ask the following questions: Does this show more monsters liked blueberry or spinach? How many votes did bubble gum get? What kind of pancakes did the monsters like least? What came in second? Discuss which chart is easiest to understand.

Page 21 Ask children to collect some data from friends or family members, such as their favorite pizza, ice cream, fruit, sport, or color. Help them represent this data on graph paper.

Page 23 Brainstorm with children other reasons people collect data, from taking a census to predicting the weather. Ask children how they would find out which flavors of ice cream people like best.